GARDEN'S CLOSE

POEMS BY
JOSEPH T. COX

Also by Joseph T. Cox

The Written Wars:
American War Prose Through the Civil War

Jan '18

GARDEN'S CLOSE

To Ryan,

My valued colleague
and dear friend.

—Joe

POEMS BY
JOSEPH T. COX

Joseph T. Cox

Thirteenth Angel Press

I gratefully acknowledge the editors of the following journals in
which many of these poems have appeared: *Antioch Review,
Black Rock Journal, Echoes: The Magazine for Creative
Communications, The New Harmony Journal, Nimrod,
Riverrun, Roanoke Review,* and *Whole Notes.*

"Miles Standish Forest, Plymouth, Mass. 1934," "Purple Hearts,"
"Shaman," and "To Send Forth," first appeared in
War, Literature, & the Arts.

Published by Thirteenth Angel Press   P. O. Box 16
Lake Forest, Illinois 60045

Printed in the United States of America

Book and cover design by Chris Crosby
Inside photographs by Linda Walters
Author photo by Ansley E. Cox
Copy set in Caslon

ISBN 0-9712466-1-0

First Printing

...he knows in singing not to sing.
The question that he frames in all but words
Is what to make of a diminished thing.

— Robert Frost

for Kathy

Contents

I

Nesting

Through December's dead branches,
mallards rise from the brush-choked pond,
their circles, twice-daily rituals,
markers of approaching and departing light.

In the bare crotch of the sweetbay magnolia,
the fox sparrows' nest unravels in the wind.
They return from winters south to thatch and mend,
a process predictable, unlearned.

Great cathedrals copy ancient wood;
a stone cottage in the center of our forest
reminds us of what we already know —
amarantal tracks in first snow.

Garden's Close

It took one November Sunday to tear down
eight years of garden. Racing the frozen ground's grip,
I tugged at green fence posts and last season's stalks
until the gate alone opened to what was and never tilled.

Most of what had been resisted:
one post grown fast in hidden tree root,
like some Erin's sword, refusing to budge
and breaking deep in loam.

Raspberry tendrils held fast;
rhubarb, too, resisted leaving the deep tap home;
but wintergreen's shallow roots surrendered in carpets of scent;
and fennel, tarragon, and belladonna savored the cold air
with the balms of holidays and great homecomings.

Wary, four-hooved suitors watched from the hillside,
waiting for shadow to forage that denied them.
And as I worked, I asked why you were not by my side.
But, of course, there are things we do alone.

I will not help tear down your fences,
harrow your heart, pull your life out by its roots.
After fallow, together we will dress some new world
for flowers and stand amazed as the heart's clear cut
retimbers, refleshing the bones of a discovered land.

First Night, Vermont

We caught ourselves in each other's eyes that first night,
wordlessly comprehending the tempest,
sensing a deep derangement, desire floating on breezes
drifting through screens, overrunning our paths, entering us.

Sudden thoughts like lightning strikes in a dry time,
flames from hidden places, faces and arms glowing.
All landscape becoming longing.

We walked together on a parched path,
each sweet lift and brush of bodies yearning,
entering the pine, desire surrounding us.

Mostly faces, smiles, greetings pass like dim light,
but on our first lustrous night
the full moon touched the trees,
and all the world we ever knew burst into flame.

Two Solitudes

Love consists in this: that two solitudes protect and touch and greet each other.
— *Rainer Maria Rilke*

From my first restless toss in the morning
to the last light switch at night,
from solitude to loneliness, I look for you,
hear you rustle in the dry leaves
as the chill turns my face and the sun
slants toward the north and west.

I hold your letters,
trace the curve of your name,
wish time and distance
were empty words
without gravity and wait.

How much longer must we go on
being husband and wife alone?

Aurora

The sun is now in the most intense phase of its 11-year sunspot cycle.
— *The New York Times, July 16, 2001*

Blinking over the prairie, the sun
fills your upstairs bedroom, bathing you asleep
in yellow sheets.

                Drawn to your soft side
I lie down, miles melt into time, distance
disappears. You turn, the curves of our bodies meet.

It is a time of great storms,
powerful magnetic fields protect
and pull charged particles to the poles,
painting the midwestern sky
with silent fireworks.

Under the light quilt, all comes clear.
Imagine, northern lights this far south,
and in the middle of July.

Burning the Furniture

What did I know, what did I know/ of love's austere and lonely offices?
— *Robert Hayden*

I simply have to ask what went wrong.
Wasn't it a fine house with many closets?
True, I never looked under the bed
and counted icicles stalactiting,
nor did I feel the cold pinch
behind the frozen smile.

How do we drive out that kind of cold?
With or without words? Grudgingly tugging,
turning words into rags, tucking them into
a pathetic nest against the north wind?

Or do we simply accept that axes shift
causing whole worlds to displace their own selves,
turning heads and the very light around
in order to see it all new, to see it clearly,
grown dull and senseless, numb to soft caress?

No, the secret lies in simple acts: banking kindling
and rationing our heartwood for the inevitable cold,
and then feeding that pure fire with every goddamn stick
of furniture on which we have not yet made love.

The Thirteenth Angel

The thirteenth angel watches over my lover as she writes.
Surrounded by prairie, lost in reverie, her angel eyes reflect
the distance of mid-winter passage in Atlantic storms.

Her face bleached, fractured and cracked by heartland sun;
her wings bored, beaten to splinters by pitiless time.

My lover, the lake poet, sees a world beyond in her face,
a time when passion came home from a long journey,
an age of sacrifice, sacred dances, garlands of ivy and violet.

With her words she cures the plague that is a life
void of the heirlooms of the human heart.

Meanwhile, the remaining twelve angels adorn
a grand banquet hall in a prosperous kingdom,
but theirs is another story.

The lake poet describes Zeus and Hera making love
on a golden cloud and how the one attending angel
who dared to look was turned to wood
and banished to my lover's imagination.

Looking for Odd Jobs, Walt Whitman Repairs Emily Dickinson's Back Porch Door — May 14th, 1850

Breeze-beaten hawthorn petals collect
against the barn. You doff
your black hat, roll up your sleeves,
and start work on the bulged door.

From upstairs I watch you loaf —
pick chokecherry blossoms,
walk back and forth to the well,
and, drunk on your own perfume, dance
on thick legs in heavy boots,
mouthing an aria I never heard.

Later the plane rasps its passing breath,
the hammer, dull heartbeats.
Stillness. Your work complete.
I lock the newly-snug door and retreat.

II

Cape May Victorian —————————————————————

High in the hat turret of the Evin Tasker Hotel,
she made his body weep on sheets white
as beach sand in the moonlight,
her body as smooth as the whiskey he poured from a jar.

Alone on their small belvedere,
with the taste of her sweetness
still in his mouth,
he felt his soul turn
and drop into the sea.

Between the wars, Grant had walked this beach,
searching for solace after the death of his son.
During the day there were segregated swimming hours —
red flags for the men and green for the women —
but at night lonely couples stared at the sea,
while one drunk soldier counted the fish-scale shingles.

Miles Standish Forest, Plymouth, Mass. 1934 ——————

'Tis good for men to love their present pains.
— *Shakespeare, Henry V*

Through the sepia tones of the cracked photograph they grin,
their mufti stocking caps at jaunty angles, tilted back, off and
on the far right of the leg-crossed front row, everybody's best friend,
the company dog, guarded by a hulking pilgrim with no front teeth.

Cadre, second row center, two foresters, four regular army veterans
in Smokey the Bear hats and puttees, arms folded, grim prophets
lost in a memory of forfeited America. On the top row six cooks
in white, you dead center, your indigo eyes smiling handsome.

All this just a month before your first taste of home-made hooch
made you run in naked innocence through the cold Cap Cod rain,
a year before Mussolini became the white emperor of Abyssinia,
and a decade before your life ran russet in the snow of Bastogne.

How many others were signed to die? How many other sons
search these ignored archives for fathers they never knew?

Shaman

— for John Wolf, 2/327 Infantry

In cloud-hidden summits of the Annamese Cordillera,
your God was a local deity without jurisdiction.
Ancient game trails lead nowhere, suffocating heat,
sponge-footed slogging through leech-leafed jungle,
sudden jolts of adrenaline when the point hesitated
over sandal track, bloody bandage, or dark distant log.

Sometimes it started with the whoosh of an RPG,
sometimes with fire squalls shredding vegetation
and flesh, splintering tree and bone. Amidst red
and green tracers, a gun-smoke shadow touched
those it took when night falls and contact breaks,
and ecstatic exhilaration dissipated in silent
scenes of rubbery, skull-shattered masks,
dead boys' faces, and schemeless mutilation.

Try to hide the fear and hope for clarity as you turn
in the churning wave of hot, dry vapor. Lie
oddly joyous in blood-drenched numbness and become
the grass waving in the warm, summer breeze.
And at this point of saturation, accept his hand,
and chant that war's mantra — "It don't mean nothin'."

Geronimo

More than eighty years
after the warm springs
of the Gila River, you lay broken
in a frozen Oklahoma ditch
and died four days later,
chanting the names of faithful warriors.

Did your war begin that night
on the banks of the Janos River
where you burned your children's toys
because you could not recover their bodies
or your mutilated wife?

In the blackness, you followed just far
enough back to hear their footsteps.
Or did it begin when the voice
called your name four times,
saying, "No gun can ever kill you"?
Magic confirmed that afternoon
you cursed the soldiers' bullets and
your knife made them pray to St. Jerome.

Near the end of your life you counted
over fifty scars and repeated the prophecy,
one you believed at Ojo Caliente
when tricked by Chum, and surrendered
rather than sacrificed more women and children.

Shackled and carted in a wagon to San Carlos,
you escaped smallpox and the rope
and returned to mountain spirits and visions.

Did you dream yourself in a top hat driving
a car in Pawnee Bill's last buffalo hunt?
Or in the garden, with your latest misshapen wife,
holding the scalp of a pumpkin?
Acorns and pinon nuts,
quail and wild turkey,
giant cactus and palo verde trees
cried for your return, but in this world
even medicine men are not safe.

Purple Hearts ───────────────────────────────

In late gray light, you slide from the truck,
grimace, scowl, grimace, grimace,
dragging the bloody boot through the wet snow,
limp and limping up the back stairs.

Half your foot and four toes literally flattened
by the cast-iron stove and Uncle Al's clumsiness.
Without flinching you soak the bloody pulp
in steaming Epsom Salts, red tendrils coagulating
in your stoic's soup.

                   No house call, of course,
nor stitches, nor splint, just six more weeks
of stubborn bad temper. The usual shadow.

I almost felt the thaw of pity, maybe
even forgiveness for bruises hidden under cotton,
even the dislocated shoulder we couldn't hide from her.

No, what I felt was a cliché, "What goes around . . . ."
A cold Calvin confirmation, that shared stock company
of pain, Melville's universal cuff come home,
a sense justice that shamed us all.

Mostly she blamed the war: their last offensive
over the frozen sheaves of the Hertigan Forest,
your unit's cowardice, you left for dead,
found by Ernest, later blinded, your only ally
to this day.

                   We all inherited the austere silence,
and the stubborn defiance that let you live.
The foot healed, and we hardly noticed your limp.

To Send Forth

In Memory of 1LT Donaldson P. Tillar, III

— *Killed in Action, 27 February, 1991.*

Remembering you when
you were my son's age
the night he told me
about your death,
I feel a father's grief.

Relaying our neighbor's
news of you, my son, my son
and you, perhaps the ghost
of what my son will become.

On the day after
the last day
of the last war,
you flew somewhere
south of Babylon.

I imagine your surprise
when you tried to see your legs
in the burning wreckage
as you sunk into the melting sand.

Notes from Ban Me Thout ——————————

Such haphazard, senseless destruction: a booby trap,
a mine, a casual rocket, an unseen sniper,
desultory violence and the random waste of lives,
American and Vietnamese, soldier and civilian,
the very young, the very old,
victims of accidents in the air,
accidents on the roads, ambushes,
and, always, a pervasive and wanton
disregard for life and property.

The teenage woman on the back of a moped
hit by a speeding GI truck:
lying face down in sticky, fly-covered blood,
hips shattered, body twisted
so that her small feet pointed up,
her dark, flitting eye the only sign of life.

The dead, dismembered Vietcong's limbs and torso
planted in Montagnard earthenware pots,
left, fly-covered, on a hair-pin turn
by the side of the road as a sign.

Two soldiers who feigned engine trouble
to stay behind the convoy for the wet of warm beer and sex, ambushed.
                        When the young Captain got
to the bullet riddled vehicle, stepped up and opened the door,
pooled guts and blood splashed over his legs and feet
and on to the red dust of the road.
The dead driver's partner sobbing a half-mile back
hiding in the stink of an open sewer.

The casually offered seat on an airplane
that would disintegrate on a mountainside,
its human freight smashed, sliced,
and scattered in the elephant grass.

And that night in Ban Me Thout, an old French hotel
with a high ceiling and empty bar,
after spending the afternoon inventorying
dead men's memories, and in the process lifting
a bottle of Jack, we sat silently drinking
neat whiskey like cowboys in a bad movie,
and up against a dark wall, Jesse tried to play
Mozart through a drunken haze
to the rhythm of the distant echo of B-52 strikes
just over the Cambodian border.

The big, balding, dirty soldier,
playing deliberate music
on a dusty, untuned piano.
Headache drunk and silent.
The smell, the dust, and Jesse's sweet notes
leaving the big room
for the night air and beyond.
Broken and dismembered bodies,
the smell of shit and gore,
tropic heat in sand-bag bunkers
but in the high-ceiling, empty hotel,
Jesse's big, dirty fingers picked
just the right small notes.

James Bond Stockdale ───────────────

Listen, hear your comrades'
muffled cries, rustling brooms,
dull taps on the prison wall —
whispers of lost civilization?

Far from the roar of the flight deck
with fireballs just behind your wing tip,
you repeat "mayday, mayday"
and blast yourself into the whipping wind.

Tumbling, turning in deathly quiet,
sudden scattered rifle fire, shouts,
the mob, the savage beating,
aircraft noises fading overhead.

The ringing in your head, a shattered,
bent knee, a useless left arm:
naked, crippled — alone but for
Epictetus and your own proper good.

Years later, befuddled, blinking,
self-consciously caught in the glare
of TV lights, out-flanked
by practiced passionate intensity,

your plea for "unity over self"
an anachronism lost in the din of carnival,
lost to those unable to hear the echo
and too pampered to break the code.

Where was the hidden message
in the way you held your hands?
What secret code translated
your blinks in the bright lights?

Knowing that lameness is an impediment
of the body but not the will,
you adjusted your glasses,
and refused to bow.

Kosovo

Up a narrow road in that season made for coals,
a pale lantern swings from gate to gate
and the thin sound of a small bell tolls.

One man guides a horse-drawn cart
loaded with cumber dusted with lime,
a glowing Charon all phosphorescent,
freighting dead weight in a deadly time.

Past shadowy men playing dominoes in lamplight,
drinking heavily to forget their crime.
Past shattered icons of random blight,
a barking dog, a boy who tries to hide,
in a faint miasma of carbolic in fading light,
a mother's bare feet jostle stiffly side to side.

Looking for villains? Take your pick;
no rules apply to the cleansing of the ethnic.

III

Hour of Lead

On a page following marriage announcements,
the paper lists obituaries in five mannered paragraphs,
alphabetical family names, the details of resting in peace.

Even your picture makes these hours of lead no lighter.
Words cannot replace lovingkindness, rekindle that sparkling
ember of your grin that warmed all our collective soul, or describe
your blue eyes that saw only the best in each of us.

Mike, we lost our chief, our dean, our very best man,
our leprechaun of love. Even after twenty-five years,
too little and too lately known. Somewhere your soul
fragments are made whole again, your pain transformed
into a very bright light in a distant hall, brighter and warmer
than this April sunshine into which you vanished.

Camp

Year by year, from lack of use,
the trail narrows and will someday vanish,
but today a blue-iced, gashed
reminder of winter's rough work
leads to camp, a reclaimed shack
with new green timbers that freeze,
expand, and pop in air so cold
I feel broken glass in my nose.

Sheltered from a chilblained wind,
I stare out a frosted pane scavenged
from Grandma Peay's smoke shed
and remember Indian summer sun
baking the grimed glass until cured ham
permeated the dusty cabin.

Two days before, Dr. Brighetty,
late for class, a covey of interns in tow,
made his little speech, offered me
his condolences, and turned off the machine.
I put my head on your still-muscled chest,
held your cold, hard hand, and watched
it slowly change color.

Now, among memories of pancakes,
pinochle, and butter-fried trout,
I carefully tepee kindling and blaze
the wood stove with a single match.
I pump the hissing lantern, flinch
at its whoomp, and watch a widening
white ball burn away the shadows.

As the coffee cup warms my hands,
and large snowflakes melt on the tarpaper roof,
I stretch my numbness toward waxing warmth,
and try to remember the moment sadness took over.

Adoration

For rose-moles in all stipple upon trout that swim.
— *Gerard Manley Hopkins*

Just about when coltsfoot is in full bloom along Callicoon Creek
and wild leek sward smell is so strong it makes my eyes water,
I cross those dry woods to overhung sections that resist
summer's heavy heat and beat my way down past log jams
to undercut banks and deep holes where native bows reside.

I search out that single place a mile south of where the north branch
hurtles the main stem, and there find a place you might dream,
a pool where on still summer evenings splash after splash
of rising trout backs beneath moon-blanched boughs recall
the sea of faith and infinite symmetry.

On this minion summer day,
I carefully approach the dark swirl depth, cast the long line,
watch for the rise, and feel an electric shock of broad fin rush
for freedom. While my rod bends and bends and I play the line
like rosary beads, I stand adazzled, dumb, and dim,
remembering most of what the Jesuit juggler praised in dappled things.

Subterranean Umbra

Under the rocks are the words, and some of the words are theirs.
— Norman MacLean

As evening slants
through second growth hemlock,
a marsh hawk's wide gyre touches
more than strength;
shadow and light coalesce
in deep current spread dark.

Small rings rise to meet a singing loop,
mid-stream a yellow hackle
vanishes in heavy splash
trailing halos of amber
and honeyed spill.

Seek in this last blink
of the sun's eye,
beneath the full flood
of the Neversink,
reflections in timeless
geography, black stones,
and brown trout.

Ultralight Spinning

Far from the drone of distant highways,
moss-lined pools set in hemlock silence,
hidden pools, small water and brookies,
and the shadow of a kingfisher moving
off into far hills of land and height.
It made his heart tighten as they moved,
and he felt all the old feeling. Hazy,
black-plum flanks, vermilion dots
laid on fields of lavender blue,
snake-like vermiculations of green,
pectoral and ventral fins edged in ivory.
Not a trout at all but a char, painted
by the hand of Zeus to shame all other fish.

Black Rock Forest ────────────

These are the first days back there,
along our woods' main path now full
of summer musk, slanting light,
and scurry sounds of birds
before they begin to sing.

Full, too, of deliriant laurel,
torpid pockets of fragrances,
smells too sweet lingering in
damp air strangely sedentary.

At the place where paths cross,
the fallen white oak, limb-lopped,
broken-boughed emblem
of our hard winter's storm.
I start to talk to you, get a grip,
pick up the pace, and stare
at the pale blue sky.

Invisible morning stars turn and turn,
and love goes on grinding on its axis.

Winter's Tale ——————————————————————

Not far along the path
tracks lead to a scene
of savage clamor marking
Antigonus's first steps to eternity.

While the beautiful princess,
entrusted to destiny and shepherds,
full of the country's
midland learning,
bears all, nobly.

Snowflakes echo in the woods;
the cold stone moves.
I take your hand,
worth and honesty
justified in silence.

Shambling the Black-Braided Wale ─────────────

Each lonely scene shall thee restore.
                    — *Spencer, The Faerie Queen, 2.12.27*

Meanwhile, the weary Chola widow,
sits mottled under a prickly pear,
selling slogans:

> *The eye is not satisfied by seeing.*
> *All is a striving after the wind.*

and her favorite:

> *To live is to suffer*
> *but to suffer is to endure.*

We might wonder how many moments
of glad grace they knew?

Or how helpless their hearts
held what most will never know?

But now, he is an old man
in midwinter wandering frozen mountains
trying to pick flowers for a woman
who thinks he is dead.

IV

A Place Not Known by Sight

There is nothing poetic about the soybean,
that most practical fruit smugly feeding the world,
but at the edge of that dryness begins
a path pillowed with fallen needles leading
to a molted cabin surrounded by daffodils
spread like a tablecloth under thin pines
humming in the wind.

        And beyond,
over the hill at the end of the abandoned trail,
lies the clear water, a blue bottomed lake
they call it down here, fed by springs deep
in pickerel guarded weeds, a world darker by far
than the sun baked soybeans and dancing daffodils,
a stygian mire where nothing more descends.

The Smallest Sense

Sometimes we dream dreams inside of dreams
from which we never want to wake:
when we kissed, I tasted something
I needed to live, and when I held you close
in the steep hours of morning, my heart was fully still.

Sometimes we dream dreams inside of dreams
from which we cannot escape:
when we kissed, I tasted only
tears, and when I tried to hold you close
in the cold morning, my heart bumped and bangled.

Sometimes we dream dreams inside of dreams
from which we never return:
when we kissed, I could not hold you
nor make the smallest sense of my heart
as I watched it moving far, far away.

Wish Bringer

One day last week all the poems
you wrote me mysteriously disappeared,
vanished without a trace,
your stories about classical lovers,
their forests, their goat songs,
their suffering timeless,
even to constellation.

All that was left in the lower drawer
was this brown and black pen,
with its alchemy
against evaporating words,
a talisman that reinvests
stories with love,
with knowledge
as clear as the cold north sky,
decisive as the period
at the end of this thought.

Moonlight Graham

Once the land touches you, the wind never blows so cold again.
        — Moonlight Graham to Ray Kinsella in Shoeless Joe.

A remote glade, a wooded break,
the mirror surface of a clear, black lake,
wisps of smoking, racing mist,
these few abundant places exist

where returning to secerned bower
the barred owl barks night work over,
and awakened by that hunter's cry
a blue heron silently sweeps the sky.

Our breaths consort in cold, matin air
and evanesce in the sun's cautery glare.
We wake to every day's delusory dream,
but in hallowed places our lives redeem.

Dog Prayers ───────────────

That woman across the street
called the cops again to complain
that my backyard barking was indiscreet.

I would like to chain her near
and see if she could resist harmonizing
with fire trucks we would hear.

See if she could stay
a mournful resonating, chord-on-chord
when sirens mark the middle of day.

See if she could control the yawll
of bitch heat in summer air.
See her try to heel her tongue
when moonlit ancestral echoes call.

May there be fat cats in the four corners of her yard,
may her collar be too tight,
May her chain confine her to piss burn,
and may neighboring dogs come only to bite.

Lovemunk

Not quite born between two worlds,
but almost, and in a lesser fashion,
I have my father's gray,
but barely half his tail, tinted rust.

Neither squirrel nor chipmunk,
conceived under the cold moon's glare,
in a rustle of odd animal necessity.

What broken rules,
what betrayed feral instincts
inspire this love-child lyric,
and what retribution attends?

Bah! gods, stand up for lovemunk!
May he grow and grow,
vaster than empire but more slow.

Baseball Reflections at Middle Age ————————

Imagine that singular last blink of a star
centuries dead, its cold light solitary
traveling void toward oblivion.
Imagine, too, the last flash of a common firefly
turning out the lights of summer.

Somewhere in this equation,
somewhere between the sweet smell
of first cut grass and that last firefly blink,
competing with sound of ball on bat
are distant truant voices,
a diaphony reaching our ears like last star light,
even as those who spoke are forever far away.

7

Poetry Dog

A few years back one of TV's more poetic commercials claimed, "Dogs love trucks!" and the commercial left you believing they really do. This essay is my commercial for poetry. "I love poetry!" and hope you read this essay and believe that I really do, and that you should, too. Loving poetry is something most retired professional soldiers and current Heads of schools, hell, most normal people, don't advertise, but (as some will argue) poetry might just save your life, tell you the news you can't find in the paper (or at least help you make sense of it!), and it can be fun in the process.

Most on this planet believe poems are about as useful to people as trucks are to dogs. Poetry and poets inspire "deep thoughts" and a lot of what passes for poetry stinks worse than dog doo; yet, according to Robert Frost and others, good poems "take life by the throat." Somerset Maugham claims, "The writer of prose can only step aside when the poet passes." Poets are the Alpha dogs of writing, but what they write helps the pack. John F. Kennedy (who, it seems, knew a thing or two about being an Alpha male, but, more importantly, knew poetry too) says, "When power narrows the areas of man's concern, poetry reminds him of the richness and diversity of his experience. When power corrupts, poetry cleanses."

Some other barbaric yelps: "Poetry is a perfectly possible means of overcoming chaos." "Poetry is the language in which man explores his own amazement." "Writing poetry is to hold judgment on your soul." HEAV-VEE! What I want to tell you is that poetry can tell you the truth about some things, can make you see and think about what it means to be a man or a woman in ways that help you appreciate what we all have in common, and, on special occasions, can and will make you feel like the top of your head just came off (Emily

Dickinson made up that one). Good poetry is man's way of barking at the moon.

But, really though, why DO dogs love trucks? The commercial would have us believe they like the way trucks look, all shiny and sleek and powerful. They like to go for rides and hang their heads out the window and let their ears and the slobber from their tongues blow in the wind. They like to yap at other dogs along the way and just bark to hear themselves bark. Hell, dogs enjoy life; they like the ride; and they like your company. Poetry can do that for you, too. There is the form to admire, the way it looks, its image and color, the sound of the engine, the hiss of the wheels on the highway, the wind in your hair, the getting from here to there in style — and **fast**! The images racing by, the people you meet, the sense of having tasted life.

As we take this ride, different dogs will see different things, and each will have its favorite truck or, for that matter, fire hydrant. Jump in the flatbed of contemporary American poetry; get in the back seat of a European touring car; try a horse and buggy of a century gone by. Take in a poetry workshop. Walk your walk and perfect your bark by sharing your work with the pack. Along the way you will be better off for meeting the top dogs of poetry. I really do love poetry.